M.L. Stanford

They Used to Call Me Pinky

THEY USED TO
Growing Up in

CALL ME PINKY
America's Heartland

BY

M. LYNN STANFIELD

WRITER'S PROOF

Published by Writer's Proof, a division of Interview You, LLC

Athens, Georgia

www.interviewyou.net

Copyright © 2006 by M. Lynn Stanfield.

All rights reserved.

Cover design by Anna Poyner.

ISBN 0-9773365-3-0

Printed in the United States of America

DEDICATION

To my family, my country, and my God.

THEY USED TO CALL ME PINKY
Growing Up in America's Heartland

M. LYNN STANFIELD

Introduction	*xi*
1. How I Got My Nickname	*1*
2. Early Memories	*5*
3. My Stanfield Education	*9*
4. Now That's Entertainment!	*15*
5. The Huckster Wagon	*21*
6. Fear Grandma and Other True Stories	*23*
7. Driving and Riding	*29*
8. Skinny Dipping	*37*
9. Black Gold	*39*
10. The Mighty Midgets	*41*
11. Hired Help or "There's a Rat in this Can!"	*43*
12. School Sports	*47*
13. Summer on the Farm and Walking to Needmore	*49*
14. Football, Basketball, and Mary Nell Ozment	*51*
15. My Slick Car	*53*
16. The Birds and the Bees	*61*
17. "Damn It, Pink, We're on a Time Out"	*63*
18. Water Tales	*69*
19. Farewell, Forry	*75*
20. Our Band, Dick Van Dyke, and I	*79*
21. Hiding a Car and Other Amusements	*85*
22. Separation	*93*

INTRODUCTION

My name is Lynn Stanfield, and I live in Athens, Georgia. My daughter, Sally, heard me talking with my sister and brother-in-law about living in the little town of Martinsville, Illinois, when we were young. She thought what we said was interesting and asked me to put some of those stories on paper. I have done as she asked, and I'd like to say that's the way it was, and I enjoyed it all. So, here we go.

CHAPTER 1

How I Got My Nickname

I've been Lynn since I met my bride in Texas in 1953: prior to that I was Pinky. I earned that name when I was five years old and one of my maternal grandmothers was on her deathbed in our downstairs bedroom. (We had three bedrooms upstairs: one for my parents, O. R. and Leah; one for my sister, Marian, and Aunt Fanny, when she was with us; and one for my brother, Max, and me.)

Grandma Baker was very ill. To make a more quiet and respectful surrounding, my folks sent the three of us children to the lake. I was a little over 5, Marian was 9, and Max was 14. The lake was four or five miles from town and was used for both swimming and fishing. The lake, developed by the members, who paid dues and ensured it was maintained, covered about six or seven acres and looked pretty darned big to me.

We got there early in the morning and stayed a long, long time. We had relatives, Uncle Charlie and Aunt Emma Millis, who lived behind the lake, on the next road over. During the day when we got tired of the lake, we'd trek through the woods, over the plowed field, for about a mile to Uncle Charlie's house. My little five-year-old legs were too short to keep making that trek, so the last time or two that my siblings made that trip, I just stayed at the lake. At five I wasn't nearly as smart as I am now, so I just stayed in the sun on the shore and got in the water at the shallow end when I got too hot. Since I'm very light skinned and had a reddish tint to my hair then, you can imagine the result. I've been sunburned many times since, but never anything like I was that day. I had water blisters on my back as big as quarters, and some of them were so bad they were filled with blood. My chest, arms, face, and legs were burned, too, but not as severely as my back.

That evening, the good Dr. Wilhoit came to see Grandma Baker. I was sitting on the piano bench, practicing my music lesson. As he passed by me, he reached out and patted my back. The blood blisters on my back broke, and the adults had a bit of a problem getting them to stop bleeding. They took me to the kitchen, grabbed a wash pan and put me, with the pan under my back and a wet towel to help them stop the bleeding, all in the sink. I don't remember it hurting, but I do remember all the attention I was getting. Dr. Wilhoit was beside himself and was barely this side of tears. I could tell that, and I knew that I was about to get a sucker. I was restricted to the house for a couple of days while I recuperated.

We had neighbors who owned the two houses between our house and the Pennsylvania Railroad tracks and a big barn next to the last house. They had two boys, Barney, who was about Max's age, and Allen, who was Marian's age. They kept a cow or two in the barn so they had fresh milk, and it was Barney and Allen's chore to milk them. When I was released from house confinement, I could play in the back yard. I was doing this when the two of them came by to go milk the cows. When they saw me in my new red hue, they said, "Look at little Pinky." That was the first time I was called Pinky, but certainly not the last.

I'm told that as a child my fuse was rather short, and I do remember trying to punish them with my fists for calling me that. It worried them a lot. They just put their hand on my head and let me flail away at the air. When I got tired of boxing air and relaxed a bit, they laughed and went on their way. In a little town it doesn't take long for word to get around, and within a week everyone under 25 knew I got most upset if you called me Pinky. Within another month or so the name stuck. It took a little longer for the older folks to sign on, but by the time I was in high school, even the teachers called me Pink or Pinky.

Before that, I was Merlin Lynn. Not Merlin. Not Lynn. Merlin Lynn. I accused my mother of naming me after a famous movie star, Rin Tin Tin, but she always said that Beulah Millis and Madge Arney were responsible for my ringing name.

Until my late twenties I was quite satisfied to be Pink. But, somehow, I didn't think Pink looked good on a résumé, and thought a name like that might keep me from realizing my vast potential. I should have kept it. Then I would have had an excuse.

CHAPTER 2

Early Memories

One of the first things I can remember is sliding on the snow, down the hill in front of our house. I was in front on the sled and my mother was behind me, supposedly guiding the thing. I can remember going into the ditch and having Mom all over me. I wasn't hurt, but she broke her leg.

At the same house I can recall getting a "pickaninny" doll when my parents went to Mississippi to visit our relatives, the Forresters. I remember, too, getting into a 1929 Model A Tudor Ford, sitting in the back seat while Mom (all 125 pounds of her) pushed it to the top of the hill, jumped in, and roll-started it. I remember one day the car stalled just before the bridge over Little Creek, and the local vet, Dr. Harry Downey, got it going again for us. I couldn't understand why he was helping my mother, and it bothered me.

I've been told of other things I was involved in while we lived in that house on the hill, like the time I called the school superintendent "Old Horse Feathers," but I don't really remember them.

Next we moved to the house on the corner that Dwight Millis, a cousin who was always very close to our family, later bought. I remember a birthday party there, and there are pictures of that in my picture album. That's where we lived when I had my first experience with smoking. I'd pick up butts that were long enough to use and puff away. I'd filch matches at home and use them to relight the dead butts. I couldn't have been more than four, so my handling of the matches wasn't real stable. Evidently, when relighting I had burned my eyebrows. When I showed up at the store on one particular Saturday evening, my Mother asked me if I had been smoking. I was most surprised she knew, and I told her that some big boys told me that if I didn't smoke they were going to push that car over on me. When she wanted to know what car, I told her the one behind them. It was a long time before I understood how she knew I'd been misbehaving — for in our house smoking stood just behind drinking in the list of bad behaviors — or why she didn't believe me. We reached an agreement that night. I wanted heel plates on my everyday shoes; neither of my parents wanted me to have them. Our bargain was if I would not smoke, I could get heel plates put on my shoes. That agreement lasted 14 years until I entered the U. S. Army Air Corps in 1944.

That house had two bedrooms. One was used by my parents. Everybody else used the other one. It must have been pretty big, because Grandma Baker, Max, Marian, the hired girl, and I all slept there. Grandma kept a "slop jar" under her bed. She used the jar to relieve herself as needed, in spite of all the people there. I guess if it was dark enough, she had adequate protection for modesty.

At one point in time the Methodist minister's home was quarantined. The preacher had a son who was Max's age, and this son was not at home when the quarantine was instituted. So, he lived with us for the duration of the quarantine. Guess where he slept?

Grandma had a goiter (a big growth on her throat), and she'd go through a rather long and involved throat-clearing procedure when she first lay down. She'd go "Aaaahhhheeemmm," and Carl Honn, the preacher's son, would mock her. It was all we could do to keep from laughing. ("We" included Marian, the hired girl, Max, Carl, and me.)

Another memory involves our Chicago relatives. Tom Anderton had married Lois Baker. Lois was Fanny Rue Baker

Long's daughter and Grandma Baker's. Fanny was always known as Aunt Fanny, but in reality she was my grandmother. She lived with us the last 15 or so years of her life, but she never acknowledged the true relationship to any of us. More about that later. Anyway, Tom and Lois had visited for a couple of days and had used Mom and Dad's bedroom. They were packing their bags and getting ready to return to the big city. Tom had obtained one of those fake piles of defecation and placed it on top of their luggage. Everyone went into the bedroom to bid their adieus when Tom said, "What's this?" The first thing Mother did was to grab me and shake me. She was getting ready to whip me good when Tom laughed, picked up the pile, and put it in his pocket. Everybody got a big kick out of it but me. I don't recall anyone feeling sorry for me but me. I'm sure I wasn't hurt because I was used to being shaken, spanked, spit washed, screamed at, and told what pretty blue eyes and long eyelashes I had. They all meant about the same to me.

STANFIELD'S STORE IN THE 1940'S – MARTINSVILLE, ILLINOIS

From left: My father, O. R. Stanfield, holding the Blunk child; Wilbur Deahl; the butcher, George Storzham; my uncle, Jim Stanfield; Mrs. Blunk; and Mildred Wells.

For a larger version of this photo, see pages 96 and 97.

CHAPTER 3

My Stanfield Education

Perhaps I should set the stage a little. Martinsville is a little town in east central Illinois that has been stable as long as I can remember. When we had the celebration of its first 100 years and put the big rock with the plaque on the campus of the high school, Martinsville had 1,206 residents. That was in 1934, I think, the same year that Chicago celebrated its first 100 years with the World's Fair, the Century of Progress. On each census I've looked at since, the population of Martinsville has been within 30 of what it was in 1934. It was originally a town that successful farmers moved to when they retired. The industrial base was supplied by the Pipe Line, a division of what became the Marathon Oil Company, and the line crews of the Pennsylvania Railroad. The town was a hub of sorts, and on Saturdays, the farmers for miles around came to town to get their provisions for the coming week. Not everyone had cars then, and most of the farmers came to town in a horse-drawn wagon. They tied up their horses and spent the day shopping and visiting with friends.

There was a Methodist church, a Baptist church, and a non-denominational church called the Bible church. There had been a Christian church, which didn't make it past the depression; that turned into City Hall. And on the south side of town there was a holy roller church. There were two elementary schools, one on the north side of town and one on the south, and one high school. It was appropriately named Martinsville Community High School. My last two years in high school, we even had school buses to bring in the kids from all the outlying areas. Some people rode the bus more than ten miles each way.

There were two drug stores, and eight to ten grocery stores depending on the year. There had been two banks, but one didn't make it out of the depression. Service stations had not been devised yet, but we had six to eight "filling stations." We had two feed stores, one ice house, two blacksmiths, and two hardware stores. There was at least one undertaker, one resident artist who taught violin and brass instruments as well as playing violin, a prominent piano teacher, several insurance agents, and two lawyers who had been very prominent until they had been overcome by drink or the Chicago Mob. It was in fact, a "going Jessie," and about as dynamic as a community of 1,200 people can be.

My father, Ova Roscoe Stanfield, had been principal of one of the local schools. He had a job offer for a position in Charleston, Illinois, which he accepted. The local people threw a party for my family and brought gifts. My parents were so touched by that gesture that they decided to stay in Martinsville. Dad bought a grocery store, and that decision decided a way of life for two generations.

When I speak of the store, I'm speaking of Stanfield's, where I learned almost everything I know. We sold groceries. Canned goods. Pepper, pinto beans, red beans, navy beans, salt, lard, peanuts, cookies, eggs, sugar, potatoes, tea, and crackers. These were all available in bulk. In season we had watermelons, cantaloupe, peaches, and any other thing you could stack up or put in a bin.

At some point in time Pop decided that business would be better if we sold fresh meat, so he put in a meat department. We did it all. Dad would go out to the nearby farms and buy beef and hogs. We'd send the butcher and Luke, our one-eyed shooter, skinner, and poultry dresser, out to the farm where the steer was. They'd shoot it, skin it, disembowel it, cut it into quarters, load it into the delivery truck onto cardboard that was placed on the floor so the beef wouldn't get dirty, and take it back to the store. The beef would be placed in the walk-in cooler to chill out and age. It took about four days for this to happen, so we had to have a lot of beef around all the time.

Hogs were different. With them, we had to bring them to our slaughterhouse. There we had a stall to put a steer in, where he would stand to be shot and have his throat cut. Another stall was where we ran the hogs before we either shot them or knocked them in the head. Then we made a small slit in their throats to bleed them and get the blood out of the meat. There was a vat of water about six- or seven-feet long and about two- or three-feet deep which was put over a fire. The water was heated until it steamed just right; I don't remember what the temperature was, but I'd guess about 135 degrees. After the hog quit bleeding, he was dunked in the hot water and brought up to be scraped. We had bell-shaped scrapers with handles jutting from the deepest part of the bell to remove the hogs' outer layer of skin and hair. If the water temperature was just right, it was an easy job. If it wasn't, it was a hard job to get that epidermis off.

Dad had an uncle, Charlie Cornwell, who had a dry goods store. He sold piece goods, shoes, dresses, men's and women's clothing and work clothes. His store occupied half of the front or public area of Stanfield's. It was, of course, called Cornwell's. Uncle Charlie decided to quit in the early 1940's, so Dad bought him out.

Miller's had for 40 or 50 years been the biggest store in town, but now we were gaining on them. We now could outfit you and feed you, and you wouldn't even have to leave home. We offered credit. We delivered to your home twice each day. Once in the morning, and once in the afternoon. You could charge anything we sold, and you could place orders over the telephone. Our telephone number was nine. Yes, just one number.

When I say that the store was a way of life, I'm very serious. You started working at the store when you could see over the counter or whenever you started to school, whichever came first. Part of the reason for that was Mother was in charge of posting the charges and was pretty much a fulltime employee. If we were at the store, we had a lot of people watching us. From our point of view, often there were too many watchers.

It was just a store, but to many of us it was an institution. It opened at 7:00 a.m. and closed at 6:00 p.m. Monday through Friday and was open from 7:00 a.m. until 9:00 p.m. on Saturday. On Sunday Dad would go down and open up at 8:00 a.m. and stay until 9:00. He had to leave then because he was Sunday school superintendent and had to be at the Methodist church by 9:20 to make all the announcements and lead the singing. We lived just across the street from the church, and when the bell rang, we went to church.

Back to the store. From the time I was six and going to school, Dad would wake me about 6:00 a.m. and say, "Time to go, Sprout." I'd get up, get dressed, eat breakfast, and go with him to open the store. My job was to move all the milk bottles that people had brought in the previous day; I had to take them from the front of the store to the back. Some of you readers might not know what a milk bottle is. Before we had all the prepackaged things, milk was sold in quart bottles. When you bought a quart of milk, you had to bring your bottle in exchange, or the price of the milk went up ten cents. Since the milk was only 15 cents, that was a substantial amount.

The back room was the storage area where we kept the bulk part of our stock and our kerosene, vinegar barrel, and egg-candling department and where we bought chickens, hens, and eggs.

When I could swing a broom, I also had to sweep the aisles and the sidewalk in front of the store. If I had any time left, I would straighten up the shelves. Sometimes we wouldn't have enough stock to fill the shelves, so we'd bring the cans we did have up to the front of the shelf so it would look like we were loaded.

Buying groceries was different then. The customer would enter the store, and a clerk was supposed to be right there before the customer took five steps. The customers walked to a counter and told the clerk what they wanted. This was written on a charge pad, and when the customer said he or she was through, the clerk would go all over the store and pick up what the customer wanted.

At the time, that was probably a good way to proceed, but it completely eliminated any impulsive buying. The reason it was okay is that no one had much discretionary income anyway. People had enough trouble paying for the necessities without any embellishments. And Pop couldn't afford to give any more away.

It was not unusual for the customer to get a handful of peanuts from the big jar of bulk peanuts, or eat a cookie or two from one or more of the twelve or so kinds of cookies in the cookie display case while we picked up their order. The only time the customer wanted to be with you was when you were getting meat.

Meat wasn't pre-packaged then, and there would only be a small representative sample displayed in the meat case. If what was shown didn't suit you, you'd go to the walk-in cooler, bring out the piece of beef or pork you wanted, put it on the block, and cut it to the customer's taste. I can still remember when I asked one customer who was always rather gruff how he wanted his steak cut, thick or thin. "Yes," he said, "that's the way I'll get it anyway."

And I can remember eating baloney one day when the Swift meat salesman came in. He asked me if I liked baloney. When I answered yes, he told me what they made baloney out of. It was years before I could eat baloney again. Then there was the day when I was eight or nine and waiting on a customer who was always a little light fingered, counting out her change. She looked at it a long time, counted it again, and said," That is just right, young man. You be more careful next time."

CHAPTER 4

Now That's Entertainment!

I grew up during the depression. Born in 1926, I wasn't old enough to know what was happening in '29. I certainly knew what was happening by the mid-thirties. Our family didn't have much money, but hardly anyone else did either. The only truly rich people were the Snavelys. Their father had bought some land in East Texas, and on his deathbed he beseeched them not to sell the Texas land. They kept it, and it turned out to be in the middle of the very rich East Texas oil fields.

Edgar Snavely quit selling shoes. Chester quit selling furniture. And their sister and brother-in-law quit working, too. They devoted the balance of their lives to living the good life as they thought people of wealth should. They became movers and shakers in the Bible church, and ultimately good customers of Stanfield's.

It was essential to create your own entertainment back then, and the merchants played a great part in the town's activities. Fast-pitched softball was very popular, and almost every little town had its own softball team. The merchants and the pipe liners – those people who were employed by Illinois Pipeline, which later became Marathon Oil Company – installed lights at one end of the football field at the high school. That gave us a lighted softball field. The concession stand's profits helped pay the light bill.

The local team played two or three times a week, and they won many more than they lost. I can still remember Earl Smith, who had to be close to forty, batting left-handed. He could hit the ball a mile and won many games for us. George Decker, a local boy, had left for the greener pastures of Chicago, and he brought a team from there to play us. Since Chicago was about 200 miles away, that was quite a big deal, and the whole town talked about that for a week.

Everyone followed high school athletics, too. We had football and basketball and, some years, track. Church socials, ice cream socials, cake walks, Halloween parties, Saturday night talent contests, and church talent nights were other ways we entertained ourselves. Families, even extended ones, shared what they had and met once a week for a big dinner.

On Saturday nights during the summer, before the Mars Theatre came to town, the merchants would have one street blocked off, and they would show a movie. They just set a screen in the middle of the street and ran the movie when it got dark. There were no benches or seats. If you had a folding chair, you brought it. Most of the kids who watched sat on a brick or a board or a box. If you didn't have any of those, you sat on the street. When the movie was over, you were supposed to take your seat with you. That was only common courtesy.

The town cop was Shep Doran, and he was a bit of a character. One Monday I was walking down the street, and Shep thought he would play a trick on me. He collared me, took me by the shoulder, and walked me to the jail. When we got there, he told me that I had left a brick in the street at the show on Saturday and that I'd have to stay in jail for that. He locked the door and left. I yelled and screamed for a while and probably cried. When I didn't seem to be making any progress, I quit. I decided to get old Shep in trouble. He came back after a few minutes and offered to release me if I would promise not to leave any more bricks in the street. I told him I wasn't going to get out, and he couldn't make me. When he started toward me, I would scream really loud. The upshot of the whole thing was he walked the half block to the store and told Mother that I was in jail, and he couldn't get me out. My mother, like most mothers, took great exception to anyone mistreating her own, and she wasn't too fond of Shep anyway. Mother had Parkinson's disease, and the palsy in her right hand was much worse when she was perturbed or excited. Now she was both, and I'm told that she looked like a left-handed banjo player. The problem was resolved rather easily. They sent brother Max down to get me. He didn't have any trouble. When he said, "Let's go," I did. I knew what he could do, and he was much more frightening than the cop.

As kids, we made our own toys. We made skateboards with a three-foot length of a two-by-four, an orange crate, one skate, and a one-by-two. Orange crates were made of wood then and, I guess, were made to hold one bushel. They were about thirty inches long and had two sections. The ends and the middle were made of a one-inch board that was about fourteen inches square. There were two thin boards about one-quarter-inch thick, six-inches wide and thirty-inches long on each of the four sides. By the time we got them, the two boards on the top of the crate had been removed so the oranges could be taken out. We'd nail half of the skate to the front of the two-by-four and the other half to the back. We'd nail the orange crate to the opposite side of the two-by-four from the skate in the front, and the one-by-two would be nailed to the top of the orange crate to give us a steering handle. Those things would really scoot, and if you were careful when you made them, would last a long, long time. We'd have races, play follow-the-leader, and sometimes have ten of us in a row riding those and kicking our way down the street.

Another thing we did was make racers. If you had four wheels and some boards, you were in business. As our experience and intelligence increased, our cars became more sophisticated. We started with rope steering, and ended with steering wheels, brakes, springs, and a couple of kids even had motors. Powered mobility.

Rolla Burger ran the hardware store that we patronized. The

Burgers were friends of my parents, went to our church, and were in Eastern Star and the Masonic Lodge with them. Any questions I had that involved mechanics were answered by Rolla. I'm certain he tired of answering stupid questions, but he never showed it, and he helped many of us discover how to plan and think. We occasionally had Sunday dinner with them. On one such Sunday, we were at the Burgers, along with the Arneys. The Arneys had a little girl about a year younger than me, Joanne. We were playing in the yard, Joanne and I, when she took exception to something that I said or did. I don't know what occasioned it, nor am I sure I ever knew. I looked around and she was charging me with a hatchet. I was a little bigger, a little faster, and a little louder than she was. I used all those superior talents to get up a little tree and scream for help. She never forgot that, and 30 or 40 years later if we'd meet, she'd remind me that she chased me up a tree.

When I was eight or ten, they tore down an old house that was across the street and up a hill from home. When they cleared up the mess, they left a pile of boards, a couple of small windows, and a closet door about four feet high. My closest playmates were the Greenwells: Janelle, Don, and Norma Jean, who, for some reason, we all called Geece. The four of us dragged some boards, windows, and the door down by the mini-creek and built a frame for a playhouse. We had the windows and the door, but we didn't have enough boards for the sides. When I came home from the store, I dragged two or three big cardboard boxes home with me. We flattened them out and covered the sides and the roof with that. We could see out, had a door, and were playing in tall cotton.

It was the fall of the year, and it was cool. So we built a stove. Down the alley less than a half block away was a garage that the State of Illinois Highway Department used to store provisions and trucks. They had some metal barrels about two feet high and about fourteen inches in diameter. These had originally had tar in them that had been heated and then poured into cracks in the highway. These barrels had a knockout in the top of them about six inches in diameter. We found an empty one, knocked a big hole near the bottom so we could feed the fire, found a piece of stovepipe, and installed our stove. We ran the stovepipe through our cardboard roof and had the stove less than a foot from the sides of our house.

I came home for lunch – it was a Saturday – ate in a hurry, and charged across the street to our house. Don and Janelle were there, so we built a fire in the stove. We were, as my Dad often said, as snug as a bug in a rug. I stayed as long as I thought I could and then went back to the store.

A short time after I had returned to the store, Pop came to me and asked me if I had been playing across the street at home when I went to lunch. I told him that I had, that we had built a play house and had built a stove. "Well, you won't play in it anymore," he said. "The fire department just had to put out the fire in that field and in your playhouse." That was the last house I ever built of cardboard.

There were telephone poles in that field on a rack. I don't know who they belonged to, but they were obviously stored there in order to be used as needed. They gave us a haven and a place to play where we couldn't be seen by any prying eyes. We played there a lot, and that's where the Greenwells and I learned the delightful difference between boys and girls. At first we reveled in our new-found discoveries, but it didn't take long before it was more fun to shoot rubber guns than to look and explore.

CHAPTER 5

The Huckster Wagon

Earning a living was no easy thing before the Depression and much harder during it. You had to muster and exercise all the initiative you could find. Some of that initiative, as far as the store was concerned, involved a huckster wagon. Most people didn't have cars, and if you lived out of town, your transportation was by horse or horse and buggy or wagon. Consequently, people didn't go to the store on a whim to pick up something.

My granddad, Otto, would load up the wagon and go through the neighboring countryside, stop at every house, and ask if the people there need any provisions. He had regular routes and got to know the people and their needs. If he didn't happen to have what they wanted on one trip, he'd put it on the wagon for his next trip there.

Before the Depression, many young men aspiring to better themselves left Martinsville for the big cities. Many did well before Black Friday in 1929. Then those young men found that Martinsville was the only place they could sustain themselves and returned to their old homes. One of these returnees built a nine-hole miniature golf course on his family's farm a short distance from town.

He ordered some groceries and asked if we could deliver them. Dad said we could, took the order, filled it, and sent Granddad out with the order in the huckster wagon.

Granddad delivered the order and came back. "You know

what McNary's got out there?" he asked. "A nine-hole golf. What the hell's a nine-hole golf?"

❊ ❊ ❊ ❊ ❊ ❊

The huckster wagon must not have been too profitable because, eventually, he and my dad decided to stop providing the service. Or it could be that Henry Ford and his cheap cars caused the demise.

CHAPTER 6

Fear Grandma and Other True Stories

My brother eventually became a big college man and was a real hero to all of us. One Fourth of July he made me one of the most exciting toys I ever had. He took a piece of one-inch galvanized pipe, threaded one end, and screwed a cap over the threaded end. He drilled a hole in the center of the cap, and this completed his firecracker gun.

Corncobs were readily available then. Whit Wells had a feed mill next door to our store, and he always had a pile of cobs from shelling corn. They were left for anyone to use. Some people used them for fuel, and many people used them as stoppers for bottles and cans. At any rate, there was always a pile of cobs at Whit's.

This is how the firecracker gun worked. You'd take a firecracker, stick the fuse through the hole in the cap, stick a cob in the open end of the pipe, light the fuse, and wait for the firecracker to go off. If you had a good fit with the cob, you could shoot that thing close to 200 feet. My mother wasn't too thrilled with this toy, so I had to be careful when I played with it.

I had lots of cousins from the Stanfield side. My grandfather, Otto Stanfield, married Effie Cornwell. Grandmother's father was a farmer who had lots of land, and as his kids married, he gave them 40 acres of land. Effie and Otto had, in order, Otha, who died as a baby; Ova Roscoe, my father; Percy Charles; Othello Rector; James Dennis; and Maxine. Maxine died at 16 of a botched abortion that was set up by Percy. I don't think my father ever really forgave Perce (as Percy was called) for that. Perce never had any children with his first wife, Mildred Chapman, and his three children were all quite a bit younger than me and were all borne by his second wife, Thelma.

Othello was called Thell. He married his aunt, who had two boys and a girl when they were wed, and they had six kids, four girls and two boys. Five of these kids were within four years of my age. Jim had four boys, three of whom were within three years of my age. So you can see there were lots of Stanfields to play with when we got together. That age differential was one that was beneficial to all the boys. The older ones showed those of us who were younger those things that boys need to be shown, and which their fathers often hesitate to show.

I remember one time when Jimmy (who in this case was the older boy) and Bill, his brother who was my age, and I were left alone in a back bedroom for a while. We dropped our pants and were each rubbing our most sensitive spot, when Grandmother came in.. To say she put a damper on our party is a gross understatement. We were startled and very much frightened when she said in quite a loud voice, "You boys put those away, or I'm going to get the butcher knife and cut them off." I can attest that there were three scared boys, and I can further state that if any of the three ever again played with that portion of their anatomy, they were quite certain that Grandmother was nowhere around.

My cousins on the maternal side were the Millises and the Bakers. The way they got to be cousins was as follows. Fanny Rue was in love with a man who seduced her. When she became pregnant, the blaggard ran to Texas and was never seen in those parts again. That pregnancy resulted in the birth of my mother.

Emma Baker was the daughter of John and Amanda Baker. When Emma was somewhere around eight years old and saw Baby Leah, she was quite smitten. She asked her mother, Amanda, if they could take the baby home with them. Amanda and John thought that was a pretty good idea, and they did bring the baby into their family. They raised her as their own daughter, and that's how I came to have two maternal grandmothers.

In addition to Emma, the Bakers had a son, Charlie. Charlie had two boys and a girl, who were all older than me and whom I seldom played with or even saw. Emma had four boys. Two, Dwight and Buell, were fifteen or twenty years older and were more like uncles than cousins. Two, Billy John and Forrest, were two and four years older, and we had many experiences together.

Often in the summer we would go down in the country to visit Uncle Elwood and Aunt Emma for the big Sunday dinner. On one of those Sundays, Buell took me out to the pasture. On the way he told me he was going to make me smart. When we got to the right place, he reached down and broke off a plant. All I had to do to be smart, he said, was to eat this plant.

I bit off a small piece and chewed one time. It was prickly. It burned. My mouth felt as if it would all shrivel up. I seriously doubted that I'd ever again be able to taste anything. I started to cry; Buell didn't want that. He explained that I had indeed gotten smarter, and he would prove it to me. He asked me to take another bite. When I refused, he said, "See how much smarter you are."

On another trip to Aunt Emma's, we found her cat had just had kittens. Mom thought they were so cute, and Aunt Emma gave her one of them. I never was much of a cat person, so I wasn't moved much one way or another. Our back porch had been enclosed, and there were windows around three sides of it. The porch was probably 8 by 16 or so. We had our ice box on the porch, and there was a table and a chair or two there also. Mom put the cat box on that porch.

Mom had just bought a new satin bedspread; it was slick like silk, only it was satin, light green and very pretty. It was her pride and joy. You have to remember that new things didn't come around too often then, and that bedspread probably represented more than a month's disposable income for Mom. The cat liked the bedspread, too, got on it and laid a cat pile. When Mom saw that she went ballistic. She grabbed a broom, yelled, "You pesky thing!" and started chasing the cat. She'd yell and swat the broom on the floor, and the cat would yowl. She chased that cat around the bedroom, through the bathroom, into the kitchen and around the table, yelling and swatting and yowling all the time until the cat found its way to the porch and out the door. I don't know what happened to the cat, but I do know that it was never again welcome in our house.

We still lived in that house – the one where I was called Pinky, which was between the Pennsylvania railroad and U.S. Route 40 – when the next event occurred. There was an alley on the north side of our house. It ran for a short city block, then turned at a right angle and proceeded up to the highway, about a half block. Granddad and Grandmother lived in a house on the west side of the alley, where it intersected Route 40.

Granddad was part Cherokee – I think he was one-half, but it might have been one quarter – but he did like the firewater. At that time Perce had a bunch of slot machines scattered about the state. He also sold punch boards where you could win lots of money if you were lucky. You'd pay your money, punch out a number, and if it was a winner, get your money from the merchant. Perce was gone a lot, picking up his take from the slot machines. He'd blow through Martinsville every few weeks and go to see his folks. He'd talk about how good he was doing, maybe have a meal, and when Grandma wasn't around he'd give Granddad a bottle of whiskey. Granddad, who a lot of people called Cooney, would hide it and take a couple or three days to drink it up. But on this occasion, he drank it a little faster and got a bit inebriated and was irritating Grandmother.

She evidently took all she could stand, got an iron skillet out, and hit Granddad on the head. He dropped in his tracks and lay on the floor. Grandma was beside herself and called my father. She said, "Ova, get over here right now. I think I've killed your father." Since they lived so close to us, it didn't take long for Dad to get there. By the time he got there, Cooney was recovering. He hadn't been killed, just stunned, and he recovered with no further complications. I'm not sure, but I'll bet he was more careful next time he had a bottle.

Grandma baked bread and rolls. She would bake a lot of bread on Thursdays, and many people would buy bread from her. Some of my fondest memories are of visiting them and smelling that bread baking. I've never before or since had such bread. It was coarse textured, and, after a day or so, you had to be careful when you held it or put butter on it because it would crumble. When they moved to the other side of town, I'd scheme to go stay all night with them, so I could eat that good bread. Often the meals would be made up of the same foods, breakfast, dinner, and supper, (there wasn't any "lunch" there). Each meal would consist of bacon, bread, and cream gravy. If there was some fruit in season, we would have stewed fruit, and occasionally we'd have a pie or a cobbler. It was all good, but the bread was something else. I bought a bread machine and tried for two years to make that bread, but I never even came close.

CHAPTER 7

Driving and Riding

In 1936, a lot of things happened. Oklahoma blew away, and it was one hot and cold year. Almost every town has a corner where those people looking for work hang out. In Martinsville that corner was where the First National Bank had been. Across the front of the building was a ledge about two feet high which extended from the door to the corner of the building twelve or fourteen feet. All the old unemployed men who had little to do would gather there, sit, chew, talk, and spit. I was ten years old and thought I was getting to be an adult. It seemed to me that people talked most about the weather. All summer long they talked about the oppressive heat, and it *was* hot. We reached 95 degrees several days and approached 100 a time or two. That winter was colder than the proverbial well-driller's posterior. I heard the same old men talking about the bitter cold. So, when I opened conversation with adults, I started with the weather. I'm sure now they all thought I was nuts.

I have pictures of my tenth birthday party. You can see the snow and the boys. What you can't see is that the temperature was 20 degrees below zero. We all played outside in the snow and chased each other around. We couldn't move too fast, though, because the layers of clothes we had on made movement difficult. When it came time for cake and ice cream, it took 15 minutes to get all the clothes off.

The summer after my tenth birthday, Dad taught me to drive the delivery truck. I was still too short to see over the steering wheel very well, but if we took out the seat and substituted a Pepsi-Cola case on one end, I could see well enough and reach the pedals, too. Back then the Pepsi cases were large enough to hide the entire bottle. They were about 14-inches square at each end and about 24-inches long.

During that summer the delivery man must have gotten a better job, because I became the delivery boy. I thought I was ten feet tall, and you can bet the farm that I honked at every kid I knew as I drove the truck by.

U. S. Route 40 ran right through the center of town, and it was a very busy road. On Thursdays the State Highway Patrol came through town and often stopped at Mauk's Drug Store for cokes. Although drivers' licenses weren't yet required at that time, you were supposed to be 14 to drive. Since I didn't look 14, Pop told me not to drive on Route 40 on Thursdays. I could cross it, but not drive either way on it.

Backing up a little, when I was in the second or third grade, I told Dad that if I had to work, I should be paid. He agreed with me and got me a time and date book. I had to record the time I worked every day in that book. On Saturday night, we would total the hours and compute my pay. My rate was five cents an hour, and if I worked hard all week, I could make $1.25. The only kids who had more coming in were the Kannmachers, who sold fresh buttered popcorn with real butter for a nickel a sack on Saturday nights.

The only thing I didn't like about the deal was I couldn't spend the money. I had to save it. For a couple of years I put my money in postal savings at the post office. They paid a higher interest than the banks did. They paid 2%. Then the government decided that they weren't in the banking business, so they stopped that program. I withdrew all my money and put it in the Martinsville State Bank. That bank became my main bank for the next 46 years, even though I didn't live there for 28 of those years.

By the time I was in the fourth grade, I decided I needed a bicycle. I had more than $45 in the bank, and bicycles didn't cost that much. We bought some merchandise from a wholesaler in Terre

Haute, Indiana, named Levin Brothers. They had a catalog, and in it they had a bike that had all the buttons and bells. It had a chain guard, head light, tank between the bars, luggage rack, and horn. It was priced at $24.75. I worked on Pop for three weeks about a bicycle. Finally, he showed signs of weakening and said he guessed I could spend some of my money for a bike. I got out that Levin's catalog and showed him that beauty. He told me to go see what Rolla Burger had. Rolla had an old plain-Jane bike that cost $27. Dad said I could buy the one from Rolla or forget it. I was probably 35 years old before I understood why I had to patronize Burger's. But they bought their groceries from us, and if we didn't scratch their back, they couldn't scratch ours. That's a very basic concept, yet it's one many people today don't understand or live by.

That bicycle gave me a much bigger zone of exploration and influence. By the time my summer bedtime was 10:30, I was big enough and strong enough that I could ride that bicycle all over town and keep on riding for hours. We used to choose up sides and play bicycle tag. The way we played, the side that was "it" had to catch you and touch you to put you out of the game. As soon as you were touched, you were gone. One dark night, and I mean the moon wasn't shining, we were playing bike tag, and I was the last man alive on our team. Bill Patchett saw me and started after me. We rode for four or five blocks, and he still couldn't catch me. He was gaining on me, and I felt that I could evade him if I rode in back of the houses. I turned up Ben Flenner's drive and rode behind Pat Anderson's house. I turned to see if Bill was still behind me. All I knew was that he was behind me, and I had to escape. I was pumping my bike, huffing and puffing, trying to stay ahead. I had forgotten, if I ever knew, that Pat had a clothesline strung in his back yard. I had just turned my head toward the front when I felt a strong jerk under my chin. My feet went up in the air, the bike kept going, and I had been put out of the game by a clothesline. Bill caught me and was just as surprised as I was that I was okay.

I'm about seven years old in this photo.

This is the program from my grade school graduation.

... PROGRAM ...

Processional

Invocation .... Rev. H. C. Munch

Alto Horn Solo, Evening Star .... Wagner
Jimmie Weldon

Dance Ye Gypsies .... Brahms

There Are Fairies Dancing on the Lawn .. Old Irish Tune
Girls' Glee Club

Address .... Mr. H. De F. Widger
Professor of English, Eastern Illinois State Teachers
College, Charleston, Illinois

Saxophone Solo, Italian Serenade .... Gurewick
Billy Kannmacher

Presentation of Diplomas and Awards .... G. W. Anderson

Violin Solo, Londonderry Air .... (Old Irish Tune)
Reba Brown

Benediction .... Rev. H. C. Munch

... CLASS ROLL ...

Jack Armstrong	Robert Keller
Harriet Baker	Wilma Miller
Lowell Bennett	Bernard McNary
Patricia Cunningham	Ruth Perisho
Bonnie Garver	Wanda Richart
Betty Lou Germain	Doyt Romines
Erma Gray	Bill Stanfield
Janell Greenwell	Merlin Stanfield
Clayton Hammond	Max Sweet
Floyd Huckaba	Jimmie Weldon
Billy Kannmacher	Grace Zachary

CLASS FLOWER
The Rose

CLASS MOTTO
Ambition's light is a distant star

CLASS COLORS
Purple and White

Class Salutatorian .... Wanda Richart
Class Valedictorian .... Merlin Stanfield

This was taken at the party for my tenth birthday. It was ten degrees below zero in Martinsville that day.

Merlin Lynn Stanfield, three years old.

Max, Marion, and I, all dressed up.

Ova Roscoe Stanfield, my father; Leah Stanfield, my mother; my big brother, Max; my sister, Marian, and yours truly, Merlin Lynn "Pinky"

Right: The Martinsville Methodist-Episcopal Church and our house were directly across from each other. When the bell rang, we went to church.

Far right: That's me in my uniform in 1945. I sent that photo home and wrote "I'm not always this wrinkled" on the back.

I'm holding our firstborn, Carter, and my wife, Shirley, is holding Richard.

Max, Marian, and I with our mother and father

CHAPTER 8

Skinny Dipping

Since Martinsville is located in East Central Illinois, it gets cold in the winter. Once in a while in the early spring we'd get a warm spell around the first of March. On one of these unusually warm days, Bill Mauk and I thought it was warm enough to go swimming. The pipe line had a steam plant that produced the pumping pressure to move the crude oil from Martinsville to Findlay, Ohio. The condensate from that steam was dumped into North Fork Creek. We were probably 10 or 12 and were smart enough to know that the water in North Fork would be warm. That was about a mile from our homes. So we rode our bikes out to that creek and walked down to the swimming hole. Since we knew that our parents would be most difficult to deal with if they knew we had been swimming, we didn't bother with swim gear. We just went *au natural*, which was par for the creek swimming holes.

The water was warm. As a matter of fact, it was too warm. We paddled around for a bit and decided to go to Little Creek, where the water would be more temperate. We got on our bikes, rode the mile back to town, then turned and rode to Little Creek. The water was much cooler, but it wasn't so cold that it was very uncomfortable. We splashed around a bit and thought we were having fun. The creek at its deepest point was about three feet deep, and we wanted some deep water. We got out, got dressed again and rode to the lake. We were a little apprehensive about going swimming in the lake without swimming suits on, but we finally decided, and correctly so, that no one else would be swimming there on that day. We took our clothes off in the dressing room and proceeded down to the water. At this point, there is a bit of difference in the memories of the two of us. I remember diving off the diving board and, once I hit the water, believing I would never draw another breath. Just as soon as I could, I removed myself from there. Bill remembers that we had to chop some ice in the shallow end of the lake to get in. However it happened, it didn't take long to have our fill of fun at the lake.

CHAPTER 9

Black Gold

About six miles west of Martinsville is a town named Casey, which is pronounced "K Z," not "K C." Between the two towns is an old oil field which was discovered before World War I and which has gone through two or three renewals. That field ran for 10 or 12 miles to the north, and as a kid I can recall the burning flares that are a part of pumping up crude oil. The crude oil is pumped up, and natural gas comes up with it. The flares are caused by the burning off of that gas. After 20 or 30 years the field didn't produce enough oil to be profitable, so it just kind of died. But people never gave up the idea that there was oil there if we could just find it.

Someone decided that there was oil a mile or two beyond our swimming lake, Lake Idle, and moved in an old walking-beam drilling rig. A walking-beam rig drills its holes by picking up a heavy bit and dropping it. It looks a little bit like a big sawhorse with a long beam suspended between the legs. The bit is on a cable, and as the beam rises, it pulls the bit up. The opposite end of the beam is controlled by a rotating wheel, and it allows the bit to drop rapidly. So the wheel turns all day, and the bit rises and falls. That dropping of the bit drills a hole. It takes a long while, and that's why they developed rotary drilling rigs. There are a lot of considerations that I was not fully aware of, such as keeping water or drilling mud in the hole, keeping pipe going down to retain the integrity of the hole, and other obvious problems. All I knew then, or for that matter, all I know now, is that the drilling rig operated by having a long arm or beam that was connected to a wheel or an axle that made it go up and down. That rig was the basis of much conversation in our little town. Many residents would drive by to watch and to pray that oil would be found.

That looked like a lot of fun to some of us, so we made our own drilling rigs. We made frames out of two by fours, drilled a hole in another two by four, put a little pulley on one end, installed that long piece on the frame, threaded a piece of rope through the pulley, and tied the rope to a sash weight. A sash weight was used to counterbalance a window, and was installed on both sides of a window so it would stay in place if you raised it. If we had the means, we would sharpen the point. Now we were ready to drill.

We'd pull the rope up and let the weight drop. It didn't take long to get through the topsoil, and then we were into clay. We'd pour water in the hole and keep on lifting and dropping. We'd work on our holes until we tired and would leave them for another time. Before I lost interest, I drilled about seven feet down. Lowell Huffman's dad, Henry, had a machine shop. Lowell's rig was considerably better than those the rest of us made, and before long he had hooked an electric motor up to it. He ran it for a while and got his hole more than 50 feet deep. He was the undisputed champ. I don't remember why he stopped, but I think it was because his hole kept falling in.

CHAPTER 10

The Mighty Midgets

At one time, there were three baseball teams in Martinsville made up of kids. The one in our neighborhood was called the Midgets. We were mostly third and fourth graders. On the northeast side there was a team called the Eagles, and up on the northwest side, Ernie Weir had a team that was called Ernie Weir's team. Ernie was the best natural athlete I ever knew. He was a great basketball player, a very good football player, and back then he could pole vault 12 feet. The only reason he didn't vault higher was he was afraid of the fall. He could throw a wicked curve and had a fastball that only a few Midgets could hit.

We, the Midgets, were quite a bit smaller and younger than the other teams, but we played them and often beat them. Part of that might have been because we had such a small strike zone that we were hard to pitch to. Most of the team could field reasonably well, two or three could pitch well, and a couple or more were good hitters. I could not throw, field, or hit with any degree of proficiency. When we chose up sides, I was always nearer the last to be chosen than the first, even when I had provided the ball. But they did allow me to play, and generally I played right field.

At the time we lived across from the church and our neighbors to the south were the Moores. One of their daughters had married a man from West Union named Fred Gard. They had gone to California to get rich, had not succeeded, and returned home. Fred watched us play ball in the street and began talking to us. He pumped us up by telling us how good we were and how he was going to help us. He was our first exposure to a promotion man, often called a con man. He convinced us we were going to get uniforms, would schedule games with the neighboring towns, and that we would be famous all over the state. That sounded pretty good to us. I don't know if he tried to get the merchants to outfit us or not, but we never got any uniforms. We did, however, play a game against Casey. I don't remember who won, but I do remember one thing.

I was playing right field, and there were runners at both first and second. The batter hit a ball to short right field. I started running to catch it, and heard a lot of "Awww's" from my team. They thought I wasn't going to catch the ball (probably based on past performances), but I fooled them and caught the ball. The runners had left the bases, and the second baseman was calling for the ball. He was probably 15 or 20 feet from me, and I was afraid to throw the ball, because I didn't know where it would end up. So I ran to second base and had a forced out on the runner who had left second for third and hadn't returned. That was a double play. But I wasn't through yet. The runner from first base had continued to second, and I beat him there. As he came into second I tagged him; I had performed an unassisted triple play. All because I couldn't throw the ball with accuracy.

I can still hear Fred say, "Old Pink had an unassisted triple play."

CHAPTER 11

Hired Help or
"There's a Rat in this Can!"

I mentioned before that we had a hired girl. Often these helpers weren't hired for pay. They were just helping out for the privilege of room and board while they went to high school. Some of these people's names I don't remember, if I ever knew. I know Dwight and Buell Millis both lived with us while they went to high school. They helped out at the store, and Buell, especially, gave birth to some interesting stories.

Then, most people did not have mechanical refrigerators. Consequently, people bought their meat and food on a daily or meal-by-meal basis. About 5:00 p.m. every day the store would start to fill with people who were buying the food for their supper. One such time when the store was packed, Buell was getting lard for a customer. We always had a 50 pound can of lard in the meat department from which we ladled out the amount the customer wanted. On this particular evening, Buell dipped into the can and saw what was obviously a foreign object. Further probing showed that object to be a rat that had stumbled into that can while the lard was still hot. Instead of getting Dad and showing him what he had discovered, he yelled out in a loud voice, "Hey, Ovie, there's a great big rat in this lard can." I'm certain that sales of lard were slow the rest of the evening.

Another time, Buell had a customer who was interested in

a pair of overalls. They weren't marked, so Buell called out, "Hey, Ovie, how much do you prong a man for these overalls?" I guess everything is in the eye of the beholder.

The hired girls were babysitters for Marian and me as well as part-time housekeepers and cooks. That was necessary when Mom was working. Some I was too young to appreciate. Here's a story that involves a hired girl named Vinie. She was with us when I was born.

The Saturday that I came into the world, one of my family's sows had ten piglets. The next day at Sunday school, my brother said he had a new brother and ten baby pigs. To his nine-year-old mind, we were all equal.

One of those pigs became a pet and would follow people around, grunting and squealing. If you weren't careful when you left the pig pen, that pet would get out and follow you. Vinie didn't like that pig, and one day he followed her out. Instead of opening the gate and running him back in, she threw him over the fence. The pig landed wrong and died as a result. My sister still has not forgiven Vinie for that.

Let's get back to Buell. When there was stock – cattle, pigs, chickens, and horses – on farms, they had to be cared for. That involved feeding and watering. Where we lived then, we had a barn, a big shed, and a field large enough to have some livestock. The well by the watering trough was about four feet wide and the water came up within six or eight feet of the top. On the well close to the house, we had a pump. On the well for the stock there was a beam above the well that had a big pulley below it. Through this pulley ran a long piece of bailing wire that had a bucket on each end of the wire. As one bucket filled, the other was being emptied in the watering trough. So you were constantly pulling on the wire to bring up one of the buckets.

In cold weather if you touch wet metal, your hands have a tendency to stick to the metal. Buell was pulling up the buckets of water, and his hands were sticking. He was just learning to swear, and this gave him a good opportunity to practice. You can imagine that he was not in the most comfortable situation with his hands sticking. To voice his great displeasure, he swore, "This is the by Goddinest well I ever damn saw. No more fit to be a well in spite of Hell." He never got over those flowery phrases: we wouldn't let him forget.

Buell was one of the only ambidextrous people I have ever known. He was, at first, like the rest of us right-handers, but he could do almost anything equally as well with his left. He built a barn on his farm, and when he'd nail the boards up, he'd use his right hand until it got tired, and then he'd switch to his left and keep on nailing. The first time you saw him do the switch, it was startling.

One thing that my Millis cousins had in common was an almost irrational lack of fear. I can't remember any time that any of them showed fear or concern for their safety.

One day when Forry, Bill, and I had gone to Terre Haute in, I think, Dwight's 1936 Ford, a four door, Bill was driving and asked Forry to slide under him and take over. Then Bill crawled out the window on the passenger side and worked his way back on the running board. He stepped on the rear bumper, grabbed the spare tire, crossed over to the bumper on the driver's side, stepped on the running board on the driver's side, and worked his way up to the window by the driver. He crawled into the car through the window, had Forry scoot over, and resumed driving. I was, and still am, impressed.

Bill retired from the air force as a colonel and had been a base commander, a general's aide, and spent one or two years in Japan. Although he was assigned to engineering, he flew more than 10,000 hours. He was, and is, a remarkable man.

CHAPTER 12

School Sports

When I was in the fourth or fifth grade of grammar school, we started a basketball team. I went out for the team and made the cut. I don't remember if there was a cut or not, and the fact that my Dad had a car and could take five or six boys with him to the out-of-town games might have been a significant factor in my making the team. The coach could take some of the boys, and with Dad going, the transportation problem was solved. I remember that we generally had no more than 12 members of the squad, and if everybody went, we'd take no more than three cars. For that matter, we were all small enough that you could get all 12 of us in two cars. We were probably no better than average, but I think we won more than we lost.

When I was in the eighth grade, the high school coach asked our principal if he would allow some of the eighth-grade boys to practice with the high school team. Our head man, who was both principal and coach, thought that was a good idea and let Doit Romines, C. D. Hammond, and me go to these practices. Practice started at 3:15, so we had to leave school early to get to practice. We really thought we were something. We were playing with the big boys, and it certainly didn't reduce our opinions of ourselves.

That coach was one of three that had the pleasure of coaching me, and he was probably the best. He was 5 feet 9 inches tall, but had very powerful legs. He had played halfback in college football and had been center on his high school basketball team. He could jump and grab the rim of the basketball goal, and he could kick it, too. I'm not certain how that helped him play basketball, but it certainly impressed those of us he was coaching.

When he was coaching us in football, he would sometimes get the ball and run through us. If we didn't tackle him, he'd berate us for letting an old man that was slow and had poor reactions run wild. If we tackled him – and he never wore pads – he would complain that we were trying to kill an old man. We were damned either way. Catch 22. His name was John Powers, and he accepted a commission in the U. S. Navy after my freshman year. After that, I never saw him again

CHAPTER 13

Summer on the Farm and Walking to Needmore

Most members of my immediate family have often stated that I was a bit headstrong when I was a lad. They are probably right. For an example, I recall an incident one summer when I was staying with my grandparents down on their farm. My cousin Jimmy was there, too, and I looked forward to a most entertaining week. My uncle Ross Cornwell had a bunch of kids: Barbara, Rex, Junior, and a couple of girls that I never really knew. Rex was about Jimmy's age, and he came over to see us and to play. He showed us things we never even thought about, with us being from the city. Jimmy was from Olney, where the population was probably about 7,000, and I, as you no doubt recall, was from Martinsville.

In the corn crib there was a new nest of mice. They couldn't have been more than a day old and were tiny, pink, squealing things. I had never seen any newborn anything, and I was most impressed. Rex wanted to kill them, but Jimmy and I didn't want that to happen. So Rex bowed to our wishes, and we left. Looking back, I'm certain that he returned later and did the job. We went over to Rex's house to play in the barn and hay mow, but when we got there, Rex and Jim changed the plan. We were going to have a corncob fight. The two of them would stand against me. They were both older, stronger, and smarter than I was. They got in the hay mow and had me stay on the ground. They threw cobs at me, and I was supposed to throw at them in the mow. I could hardly throw a cob up there, let alone hit them. I got hit a couple of times, got mad, and thought I'd get them in trouble. So, I told them I was going home. It was about ten miles to town, but I thought I knew the way. I left.

A little less than halfway to Martinsville was an old country store in a settlement called Needmore. I walked to Needmore, and, as you can imagine, I was tired, thirsty, and getting to be very sunburned. The man who owned and ran the store knew me and called Dad at Stanfield's store to tell him that a bedraggled urchin was there and needed help. I talked to Dad on the phone, and he told me not to go anywhere, that he would come and pick me up. I stayed and Dad came, and I was most happy to see him. I never heard from either Rex or Jimmy about that, but I was certain it got them in Dutch.

CHAPTER 14

Football, Basketball, and Mary Nell Ozment

When I was in the third or fourth grade, I found out that girls were kind of nice to have around, and I always had one or two that I deemed to be special. To show them that I should be considered special, too, I'd let them use my expensive pencil. I don't remember the brand name, but it was transparent, square, and there was an indicator inside that showed where the lead was. It cost 50 cents, which was a lot of money then. (To put it in perspective, our best clerk made $8 per week; the highest paid employee was the butcher, and he made $12.) Wilma Miller had that pencil much of the time, but Wanda Richart and Bonnie Garver spent time with it, too.

As a freshman in high school, I was interested in football, basketball, and Mary Nell Ozment. I don't mean to imply that those three things were all I thought about; they were not. I've always been competitive, and school was a most competitive situation. I wanted to be at the top of all my classes with the possible exception of Latin. There were several of us in the class of '44 who had, if not great, good mental acuity. Max Sweet, Doyt Romines, C. D. Hammond, Jim Weldon, Patricia Cunningham, and Don Swope were competitive, too, and we stimulated each other. Patricia was the only one who took homework with her each day, but we didn't really have to. We had at least three study periods a day, and did our homework there or in class if the teacher was bringing some slower students up to speed. There was a war going on – you know, the big one – and for a spell of six or eight months we devised codes, wrote messages in that code, and gave them to each other to decipher. But I was interested in a lot of things, sometimes even in the store. I played both football and basketball and ran track the one year we had it when I was in school. I would have played anything the school had. I played trumpet in the band because Dad supported the school, and he would let me play instead of work if it was in the interest of the school. If there was no school function, I had 20 minutes to get to the store after school was out. I generally made it, but if I was late, he seldom said anything.

Mary Nell's best friend was Ella Jane Snavely. Ella Jane's daddy, Edgar, one of the oil-rich Snavelys, had bought her a new Chevrolet convertible in 1940. It had red leather seats, was light gray, and was some hot car. We didn't double date much because Ella Jane either couldn't go out or didn't want to, but we did tool around town in the afternoon with the top down and wave at everyone who wasn't so lucky. The car wouldn't be seen as ostentatious today, but it was then. Mary Nell's father, Boyd, worked for Marathon Pipeline and during the summer of my freshman year took a job with Colonial Pipeline, a new company that was building a pipeline from Texas City to the Northeast. They moved to Atlanta, Georgia. I was quite shaken, and it took me several weeks to find a new significant other.

The telephone company's office was just across the street from the store, and on Saturday after lunch I'd go to the telephone office and call Mary Nell on the pay phone. I think it cost about $1.50, and was more expensive than a date. When I figured that out, the phone calls stopped.

CHAPTER 15

My Slick Car

By this time, Dad had upgraded our delivery truck. One of our suppliers, I think it was General Foods, had a panel truck they were interested in selling. It was a 1940 Dodge, and to us it looked new. Our old truck, a 1936 Ford, had about had it. At any rate, that truck was almost like my car. I'd drive it home every night and take it to the store every morning. If I had a date or was double dating with someone else, I'd hose out the back, load in the lawn chairs, pick up the guys, and we were ready to roll. Depending upon the year, those of us from Martinsville would stake out girls in Casey, Greenup, Marshall, or Paris. Three or four of us would load into the truck and go to the town we were hustling. One of us would get a date and then that date would find dates for the rest of us. After we had dates, we wanted a little more privacy, and the population of the truck would diminish. On future trips, only one other guy would go with me, and we'd double date.

During the summer of my sophomore year, I bought a car. Kelly Shawver was a farmer whose farm was between Martinsville and Casey, and he had a 1930 Model A Ford with a rumble seat. It hadn't run for a couple of years, and it had been in the barn. I looked at it and bought it for $75. With it I got 12 tubes and 10 tires. Cousin Forrest helped me tow it home; it wouldn't run.

Shortly after it was mine, the OPA (Office of Price Administration) restricted the free sale of tires. If you needed a tire, you had to go to the OPA office to get a tire permit. I don't remember the restrictions, but not everyone could get a new tire. All the employees at the local Marathon Station knew I had these tires, so one day Fritz Wood called me and asked me if I'd sell one of those tires for $20. I told him sure, and he said to bring it down to the station.

Some Mexicans had been picking sugar beets in Michigan and were on their way back to Mexico when they had a blowout. Fritz and I got to talking after the Mexicans left, and I hired him to spray-paint my car. He hand-sanded it and furnished the paint and labor for $20. I thought that was a good trade. Later, when I decided to overhaul my engine, I sold another tire. (I had never seen that done to any engine, but I could work on my bicycle, so I felt qualified.)

We didn't have an auto parts store in Martinsville, but there was one in Casey where I went to get what I needed. I told the clerk I wanted a set of rings for a 1930 Model A. When he asked what size, I didn't know what he was talking about. He explained to me that they came in standard, 5 thousandths, 10 thousandths, and 15 thousandths oversize, and I started to get the drift. I still didn't know what to get, so I chose the middle size. Now I had the rings; I wasn't quite sure what to do next.

My cousins Bill and Forrest, the one we called Forry, told me I had to drop the pan, remove the bearings, and push the pistons up through the block. Of course to do this, you had to remove the head. They also told me that I had to clean out the ring grooves before I put the new rings in. I went down to the City Garage, which was run and owned by Emil Romines, and asked him how you cleaned out the grooves in the pistons. He showed me a tool he called a groove cleaner and showed me how it worked. Since it was just about time for him to quit for the day, he loaned me the tool with the proviso that I bring it back the next morning. That evening I cleaned out the grooves.

When I took the tool back, Emil asked me how I was going to

get the pistons back in the block. When I didn't know, he showed me another tool that looked like a split tin can that had a bolt on the side of the can. It was spot welded on the can, and you could tighten it to make the can smaller. After the rings were placed on the pistons, you put the piston in this tool called a ring squeezer and tightened it so the rings became the same diameter as the pistons, so both could enter the block.

The other thing we had to do was to cut the ridge out of the block. As the pistons went up and down over the twelve-year life of the car, the walls of the block were subject to wear. This wear stopped at the place on the wall where the top of the piston came. From this point up, the block was still its original size. That ridge had to be cut out. Again, Emil loaned me the tools needed to do the job. Forry helped me cut the ridge, and we started to put the engine back together.

It took us two evenings to do the reassembly job. It had been a week or more from the time we started, and we were most anxious to see the results of our efforts.

The afternoon delivery from the store was generally completed by 3:30 or 4:00. That was important because we had to have the truck to pull my car and start it. I got the truck, hooked it to my car, and had Forry pull me. We pulled it up the full four-block length of Washington Street, and every time I'd let out the clutch, it would slip rather than turn over the engine. We stopped and talked about what we were going to do and pulled some more. Still the engine didn't turn over. More stopping and talking. More pulling. I was getting quite concerned because the clutch was starting to smell bad from all the slipping. Finally, after what seemed like forever, the thing started. We unhooked, and I proudly drove my jewel home. Since it had been so tight, a problem caused by installing rings too much oversized, I was afraid to shut it off, so I let it run an hour or more in the garage to loosen it up a bit. It must have worked, for I don't recall ever having to pull it again. That car was a big part of my learning cycle.

We had a two-car garage, mostly because we always had lots of stuff to store. One side of that garage generally had either storm windows or screens, boards, lawnmowers of the type that required you to push, boxes, garden tools, ladders, and other miscellaneous items, but Dad's car was the one that got the garage at night.

On one of my trips to Terre Haute, Indiana, I bought an oil filter from Montgomery Ward's. I had read in *Popular Mechanics* or *Popular Science* that filtering oil gave far longer life and better lubrication. I wanted that for my car. When I got home and tried to install it, I found out that my engine didn't have an oil pump, so there was no way to install an oil filter. Dad's 1941 Ford Deluxe Tudor, for which I had been the chief negotiator, did have a pump, so I installed the filter on it.

When Dad was in the process of trading for that car, I went to see the Ford dealer, Dwight Moody, in Casey almost every day. Most of my trips were about the new car I was trying to get Dad to buy, but some of those trips were because Dwight had a most attractive daughter named Patti. We – Dwight, Dad, and I – agreed on a purchase price of $807 for the car. Because of all my efforts, Dwight put the chrome strips on the fenders like the Super Deluxe models had at no charge, and he installed the side mirror on the driver's side for $4, making the total $811.

Another problem that showed up later with my car was that the radiator leaked. I learned rather quickly that those cans of Stop Leak that cost 50 cents were not always effective. After trying to stop the leak two or three times, I gave up on a simple fix. So for a long time I just kept adding water, which was fine in the summer, but in the winter didn't always work. That was because I had to keep adding antifreeze. In those days they sold two kinds of antifreeze. One was just alcohol, which has a low boiling temperature.

The other was called permanent because it had a much higher boiling temperature. The alcohol was cheap, but didn't last too long.

I solved the problem by draining the radiator when I came home at night. On two occasions that winter, the water froze in the block before it drained out. It broke the cast-iron head. I went down to Emil's, where he had a whole back room full of old Model A parts he was going to junk. Among these parts were old heads. He traded me a good head for my old cracked one. He came out with a little on the deal, for I had to buy a head gasket and the gasket cement to put the head back on.

Somebody told me that ground black pepper would stop a leaking radiator. We had that at the store, so I got a scoop of pepper and put it in the radiator. It stopped the leak all right: stopped the circulation, too. Finally, Emil found an old radiator in the back, and we traded for four dollars.

At that time the headliners in most cars were a light brown color. In 1940 the Mercuries had a blue headliner. I thought that was a sexy color and decided to make mine blue, too. Fritz had painted the car a robin's egg blue and the wheels bright red, so the color would fit well. Mom had an Electrolux vacuum cleaner that had an attachment for spraying. I imagine it was to spray insecticide, but I thought that if it would work with that, it should work with dye. I brought some blue Rit dye home from the store, boiled some water, and mixed the dye with it. Then I sprayed the door panels and the headliner and waited for it to dry. Looked good, but a little weak. I did it again and got the desired result.

Cousin Forry had picked up some wings somewhere, and he loaned them to me. These were glass attachments to the windows that simulated the vent windows that many cars had. I was king of the hill with my slick car with the rumble seat.

When winter came and the roads got icy, I learned to spin my car around in the street. That was a lot of fun, but had to be done away from home or where Pop could not find out that I was showboating. It did make a hit with the girls. They thought it was fun, too.

The bumpers on Model A's were made of two strips of chromed spring steel about a quarter of an inch thick and an inch and a half wide. They were quite springy, a fact that kept me from wrecking one afternoon. There was a guy from Marshall who was in Martinsville one afternoon and who we must have insulted a bit. We – I don't remember who was with me – were going to Marshall on Route 40 just past the exit from the railroad overpass where the road was like a letter S. This guy passed me and cut in, trying to run me off the road. My bumper got caught between his fender and bumper. Before I could get my bumper out, it went between his bumper and fender three or four times. He had a pretty new Ford coupe, and what he did beat his fender up pretty badly. He was a big guy named Kenny Coles, and I always gave him a lot of room after that, then and later, after the war, when I got to know him better.

One day when I was talking to Fritz Woods, the guy who painted my car, he told me how I could get a softer ride. All we had to do was put the car on the hoist, put a two by four in the center of the spring that reached the floor, and lower the hoist slightly so the springs would open up. We did that and put a piece of inner tube slightly wider than the springs and about eight inches long folded over between each leaf. We did this on both sides and between every leaf. Coil springs were just becoming popular, and every manufacturer but Ford had gone to them for the front springs of cars. You could tell the cars that needed new shock absorbers and had coil springs by watching them stop. The front end would go down and rebound two or three times. After I fixed my springs, I could stop quickly, go into Bill Deahl's restaurant, drink a cup of coffee and come out, and the front end would still be bouncing. But it was unique. No one else's car did that.

One problem with the car was that the key had broken off in the ignition switch, and all you needed to start it was a screwdriver.

There were a couple of times when I went to get my car, and it was gone. Some of my friends wanted to go for a ride, and they just took it. The gas tank on those cars was just behind and above the motor, so the gas was fed by gravity. There was a cutoff valve just inside the passenger compartment on the firewall between the engine and passengers. After I wised up a bit, I'd turn that valve off every time I left the car. For some reason whoever was stealing it never found that valve. The car would start, but it would only run a few seconds and then die. That saved me much worrying.

I learned some things about human nature in that car, too. One thing was that if you had what people wanted, you could be very popular.

It also helped further my knowledge of the wonderful difference between the sexes and of the fact that I had responsibilities. It was a great teacher.

CHAPTER 16

The Birds and the Bees

When I was a freshman, a place called The Blue Moon opened up a couple of miles east of town. It had a good dance floor, a big juke box, and sold cokes, hamburgers, hot dogs, and a few other snacks. My sister taught me to dance, and I spent many happy hours there. The man who owned it would not allow any beer or liquor in the place, and if anyone brought some in, they were asked to leave and personally shown the door. It was a great place for those of us who were finding out about our hormones to go, and I learned to be a pretty good dancer and how to dip there. It was our meeting place for after high school games, dates, parties, and hanging out.

It was about this time that I got my facts-of-life talk from Dad. One day he said that now that I was starting to squire the girls around, I would hear the big boys talking about intimate relationships. He said it was natural and just like other natural functions. It felt good when you were doing it, and when you're through, it's all done. He said, too, that I had to be careful and respect the girls and not to do anything with anyone I wouldn't want to marry. Years later I was working with a man named Ted Hardy when I was a district sales manager for the Kendall Company. We had worked our way to Jackson, Mississippi, from New Orleans and had checked into the Holiday Inn there about 5:30. We stopped at the bar and had a couple of beers before we went to our rooms. We were in the rest room relieving ourselves when I told him that story. Ted was a rather wiry man with a very dry wit. When I completed my story, Ted said, "Well, Lynn, either I don't know what I'm doing in here or your dad doesn't know what he's doing in the bedroom." That was a very short, very elemental lecture, and one that has some humor. However, it was much longer than the one I gave my sons.

CHAPTER 17

"Damn It, Pink, We're on a Time Out"

I mentioned that I was a high school athlete. I went out for football when I was a freshman and made the traveling squad. Everybody who went to practice did. I think we had 26 or so kids try out for the team. I was about 5' 11" and weighed 120 pounds. My brother Max had played end when he was in high school, so I told the coach I wanted to play end. Max had started a tradition, and like many younger brothers, I wanted to keep it going. I learned a lot that year, but not much about football.

Our quarterback was a 150 or 160 pound junior named J. D. Elmore, and he was one tough kid. He used to let me come around the end, and when I ran by him, he'd kick me in the shins with his cleats. It took almost all season before I figured out what was happening and how to stop it. He didn't just stand there and kick me. He'd pretend to roll block me and land some two or three feet from me, then throw his cleats at my shins. He didn't stop it until one day I stopped just as he threw his block, and he couldn't reach my shins. I stepped in the middle of his stomach, and we were even. I didn't play much that year. I only got in the Casey game, which was the last game of the year, and we were getting beaten badly.

Casey had just scored, and there was a time out. It was an extremely cold day, and I had on a stocking cap, ear muffs, a pair of gloves, and a sweat shirt over my uniform. When the coach told me to go in, I ran on the field, taking off as I went all the extra clothes

I was wearing. You could see where I had come from by looking at the clothes behind me. We had the ball and were in the huddle. The quarterback called the play, and I ran up to the line of scrimmage. No one else did. The team called me back. I got the play again, and ran up to the line of scrimmage. They called me back again. Again, I got the play and started back once more, when J. D. said, "Damn it, Pink, we're on a time out."

My sophomore year I played end, and started the first four games of the year. I don't remember how we came out, but I think we won as many as we lost. I got benched for a game, and I don't know why. Never did. We were in the Eastern Illinois district, and they chose an all-district team every year. I was the most surprised boy in town when I picked up the paper and saw that I was chosen to be on the second team. That was the only athletic honor I ever got, as far as public notice was concerned.

When I was a junior, I didn't play football. The good Dr. Wilhoit wouldn't sign my medical permit for football, but he did for basketball. My problem wasn't that I had anything seriously wrong, but that I had a bad back. I had hurt it playing basketball and was getting treatment for it. I hurt it at a basketball game with Marshall at Marshall. I had stolen the ball and had dribbled down to score a lay up. I heard someone chasing me, and I thought I'd get fouled and make the free throw, too. The guy hit me in the back, and I missed the lay up and one of the two free throws.

At any rate, there was an osteopathic physician in Oblong that Dad took me to, named Waters. He had a daughter that I had played with where we lived when I was three until I was five. Her name was Eulalee, and we had lots of fun together. Her father moved to Oblong and opened up his practice. His diagnosis was that I had a rotation in my lumbar region. It was rotating between the fourth and fifth lumbar. The M.D.s of the time stated that your lumbars couldn't rotate, and they may have been correct. All I know is that every time we saw

Dr. Waters, he straightened me up, and made me feel much better. That's why I was cheering for the football team instead of playing.

And speaking of cheering, my girlfriend was a neighbor and a cheerleader for both my junior and senior years. She was a cute thing, a natural blonde with curves in all the right places, and we found lots of ways to get together and play smacky mouth. We were pretty good at it, too. We practiced a lot.

When I was a senior, I moved to halfback. Back then you played both ways, defense and offense. I was no star, but I remember three plays.

The week before our first game, I twisted my right ankle. It didn't hurt, but it swelled quite a lot. So the coach would tape it up, and I practiced on it. The day of the game, he gave us all new socks. He taped my ankle, and the sock wouldn't fit over the tape and the swelling. So he split the sock and taped it on. Then the shoe wouldn't fit over all the tape, so he taped the shoe on. By this time I had grown to 150 pounds, and a little thing like tape wasn't going to slow me down.

We played the single-wing formation, and the center snapped the ball to whoever was to get it. We had a play that I had the ball snapped to me, ran to my left, and handed it off to the other halfback. Herm Shade, the other halfback, ran to his right, where I handed him the ball. We ran that play three or four times, setting up the play for me. Same play, only I didn't hand the ball off.

This was our first game, and it was against Ridgefarm, a team that was 60 or so miles away, which was a big trip for us. When we felt we had them set up right, we ran the play for me to keep the ball. I ran nearly 60 yards, dragging that taped foot all the way for a touchdown. The only trouble was that Bob Downey clipped, and the play was called back.

The last game of the year was against Casey, probably our biggest rival. Two plays are in my memory bank from that game, one offensive and one defensive. The offensive came when we were on our two or three yard line, late in the third quarter, and we were losing by seven points. I called a flat pass to me. I caught the ball and ran 97 or 98 yards for a touchdown. Guess what? Bob Downey clipped again, and the play was called back. Bob didn't have a habit of clipping, and I'm sure he wasn't out for me, but on my two chances to be a football hero, he sure shot me down. On the very next play, I called the same play, but George Harris, our quarterback, threw the ball to the wrong man, one from Casey. He scored easily. Now our one touchdown behind became two, and we never recovered.

The defensive play was in the same game. Lee Markwell was Casey's star in both football and basketball. He was their star running back. They had a play they ran to his left and suckered me bad. Not once, but twice. I felt bad that I had been faked out so easily, and really wanted to atone. I saw him start the same play to his right, and I came up to meet him from my position at right halfback. I met him just as he cleared the line of scrimmage, and I knew he felt that tackle. We were friends then and became better friends after the war. He told me that he had been tackled a lot, but that one was as hard as any he had experienced, and I think he was telling the truth.

I played basketball all four years and lettered each year. I was pretty tall for the time, could jump fairly high, and had lots of desire. In addition, our school was small; I think there were 44 in our class, the biggest of the four classes. One thing good about going to a small school is that you can do pretty much anything you want to do if you're willing to put out the effort.

I enjoyed my freshman year of basketball better than any other year. I played in the second-team games, was vital to that team, and got to dress for the varsity games, too. I was the sixth or seventh man on the varsity squad, so I got to play in those games, too. Our coach, Johnny Powers, was probably the best coach of the three I had in the four years, and what basketball I know, I learned from him.

I don't think we ever won more than we lost, but we did put the first trophy in the case in six years, and that was from a tournament we won in Greenup. We never had a true star, although we had a few talented boys.

CHAPTER 18

Water Tales

Dad was a member of the Farm Bureau for a lot of reasons, not the least of which is they had the cheapest car insurance. Some years they sponsored statewide contests. One year they held a Clark County contest at the swimming pool at Casey. I swam in some race and won, and Bill Mauk won the diving contest. The state finals were held, I think in Charleston, but it may have been in Champaign, and I don't remember either of us winning anything . But it was still quite a thrill getting to compete all the way to the state finals.

I was a pretty good swimmer, and it paid off in a couple of cases. One time we were at the lake, the Idle Hour Rod and Gun Club, for either a Sunday school class party or a Boy Scout shindig. There were lots of boys yelling and screaming, splashing water, and jumping at each other. Loring Lee Perisho – we called him Iggy – got under the raft and couldn't find his way out. He was blubbering and gasping and needed help. I was on the raft and happened to see he was in trouble, so I dove in, swam under the raft, and pulled him out. He hadn't started turning blue yet, but he did need to get the water from his nose and upper lungs pushed out.

Another time I was working in the store when a man I didn't know ran in and asked if I was a good swimmer. I told him yes, and he said, "Let's go."

We ran to his car, and he drove about halfway to Casey, then turned off the highway about a mile to a little pond. There was a boy in the pond, and no one around there could get him out. I dove in, found him, and pulled him out. We gave him artificial respiration for twenty minutes or so, until a doctor came. I didn't know the boy and never saw the man again.

When I was just a tiny kid, I jumped off the diving board at the lake, and I couldn't swim. Dwight Millis saw me, dove in, grabbed my head, and pulled me out. I still remember how my life passed before me, and it was in living color. I owed that man a lot. He was, as Tom Anderton often said, one of the two best men he ever knew, who didn't just talk about being a Christian, but rather lived it. The other man Tom referred to was my Dad, O.R.

November 2005 (from left to right) Shirley Stanfield, Preston Stanfield, Carter Stanfield, Sharon Rockholt, Christina Stanfield, Lynn Stanfield, Sally Stanfield, Richard Stanfield and Mitch Allen

Jan/Feb 2006 Marion Fitzjarrald and Lynn Stanfield

September 2005 - Lynn and Sally Stanfield

June 2006 - Lynn and Shirley Stanfield

June 2006 Richard, Lynn, Shirley and Sally Stanfield

CHAPTER 19

Farewell, Forry

By the time I reached the second semester of my senior year, I had enough credits to graduate. This came about because I had taken more courses than the required number. I don't remember what they all were, and I guess that my transcript would show them, but I don't think it makes any difference. The upshot was I felt that I might be eligible for the draft as soon as I was 18, which would be in January on the 30th. I didn't much want to be drafted in the marching army, so I wrote on the exams that I wanted to be considered for acceptance as an army air force cadet. I was accepted and enlisted. That isn't the only reason I was anxious to enlist. I was going to have an opportunity to learn to fly, and there was not then, and may not be now, anything more glamorous than to be a fighter pilot. Flying then was just not available to most people. And then as now, only a very special few could be trained to fly fighters or pursuit planes.

I was called up on Feb. 21, 1944. There is a rather moving account of that last day at home written by my Dad in a scrapbook that was put together by my Mother.

I knew everybody in Martinsville, had delivered groceries to most of them for years, and a rather large group of people came to bid me *adieu*. One man, Bob Willison, came to me and told me if I ever needed anything, just to call him, and he'd get it to me. Bob had a heart as big as Texas and was absolutely serious. He was the same guy who had a little problem of getting his words mixed up. One time there was a drive on in town to get everybody vaccinated for small pox. Bob was talking in Mauk's drug store while drinking a cherry fountain coke, and said he had taken his wife to the doctor's office and had her "vulcanized." He was the same guy who, just before sugar rationing was instituted, came into the store and bought 200 pounds of sugar, because he wanted to get some before the hoarders got it all. But Bob was a good friend, and I told him that I'd try O.R. (my father) first, and if that didn't work, I'd call him.

Those of us that had enlisted, as well as those that had been drafted from all over Clark County, were picked up in a bus. We were taken to Terre Haute, put on a train, and sent to Chicago. There we were split into navy and army groups. Our group went to Ft. Sheridan, just north of Chicago. While we were there, I got strep throat and was hospitalized for a couple of days. The group I was with was shipped out during those two days. They went to Miami Beach and spent basic training in a luxurious beach front hotel. I was sent to Keesler Field in Biloxi, Mississippi.

It took us more than two full days and nights to get there from Chicago. Troop trains were not supposed to be, and were not, luxurious things. But 50 or 60 hours going into North Carolina to get to Biloxi had us a bit concerned. We were some sad sacks when we detrained in Biloxi. There we received our basic training.

I can recall several things about that. We had a kid from Detroit who was of Chinese extraction and who had and could really play a chromatic harmonica. That was the only musical instrument in our barracks, and Chen was most popular.

We had a man who had spent two years at Annapolis, one who had spent a couple of years at West Point, and a few who had a great deal of difficulty keeping themselves out of trouble. There we learned to march, drill, and take orders, and we fired guns at the range. The first time we fired rifles, they gave us ten rounds or so to practice. After we fired those, they showed us where we had hit the target. When they spotted my target, I had 16 hits, many close to the bull's-eye. The man to my right had no hits on his target. After they got him shooting at the proper target, my score plummeted, and his showed a close grouping near the center.

We had to shoot until we qualified, and I did qualify, ultimately. But shooting a gun was, to me, like throwing a baseball; I never was sure where it was going. You had to qualify, and you fired until you did. There were three groups. The first, I think, was marksman. The second, sharpshooter. The third and highest, expert. It took me two tries, but I made sharpshooter.

While we were at Keesler, we went through classification for cadets. Cadets were trained to be pilots, bombardiers, or navigators, and we were so classified. We were put through many days of tests, both mental and physical, to determine what we should be trained to be. All of us wanted to be fighter pilots, and the stakes were high and meaningful to us. The results of all these tests were scores that we called "stay nines." You were graded from one to nine for each classification: pilot, bombardier, or navigator. If you had a nine, you stayed. If you didn't, you might not. My scores were pilot, nine; bombardier, nine; and navigator, eight.

The big air raids over Germany had just started, and we were losing a lot of aircraft and crew members. One of the last things in classification was a session with a psychiatrist. When my time came to be with him, he asked me what I wanted to be. I told him I wanted to be a pilot. Then he wanted to know if I couldn't be a pilot, what then. I said I thought I'd be a bombardier. Then he said that on those big raids, they didn't bother to bring the ambulance for the bombardiers, they just brought the water truck and hosed them out. After that brief discussion, I decided quite rapidly that my second choice would be navigator.

My cousin Forry was at Keesler Field being trained as an aircraft mechanic and was there most of the time I was. Basic trainees did not get passes and could not leave the base. So most of our visiting was done on the base. He'd come by, and we'd go to the PX, talk, and eat.

One night we did go to town. They ran buses to town from all over camp, and all you had to do was board them. They didn't check for passes on the way out, so we just got on and went to town. It was quite an experience, and I felt very mature. On the way back, they checked passes at the gate. Since I didn't have one, I got off at the last stop before the gate. I walked about a half block down the street, jumped the fence, walked a little way on the base, boarded the next bus that came by and went back to my barracks. We did this a couple of times, and I never realized then the problems I could have gotten into.

Because of our two rather experienced servicemen, one from West Point, and the other from Annapolis, we were almost self-sufficient. One of the two took us where we were going and brought us back. They had both been used to the honor system, and still operated by it. This proved to be a bit of a problem when the navy guy turned us in for breaking ranks. The result was we had to double-time march for 45 minutes. None of us was too happy about that, and some of our group gave him a G. I. bath, which was administered with G. I. soap and a G. I. scrub brush. The next day that man was shipped out to another base to continue his training elsewhere. I never knew who the instigator was, but no one got into any trouble for it.

Forry and I had always been close, and the time we spent together at Keesler Field strengthened that bond. He was the only member of our family that didn't make it back. He flew all his bombing missions over Italy and the Poesti oil fields, some of the most dangerous missions the air corps had. When he was being rotated home, his plane blew up taking off from Dakar, heading for the U.S.A.

CHAPTER 20

Our Band, Dick Van Dyke, and I

When our basic training was completed, we were sent to Northwestern State Teachers College in Alva, Oklahoma. There we went to college for one semester.

On the way to Alva, our train stopped in Kansas City, and we were given an eight- or ten-hour taste of freedom. Chicago was supposed to have been the best city for servicemen, and it might have been, but Kansas City ran it a close second. All our attitudes had good adjustments.

When we finally got to Alva, we were in for a pleasant surprise. They had just built a new women's residence hall, and we were placed there. We had lots of fun there, and I'm sure we learned something, but I don't think we learned much that was of benefit for either us or the air force. None of us had much trouble with the courses, and if we maintained at least a B average, we were permitted to march down to the little town on Wednesday evening and get our weekly haircut. That was not at the expense of the U. S. government. We had to pay. I think it was a dollar. But it was good to get away from our living quarters.

One day some of us were in an assembly hall and found a bunch of band instruments. Before anyone knew what was happening, we had a band formed. I don't remember how many guys we had, but we could play all the instruments that the school had. Our commanding officer got permission from the school to use them, and even scoured up some music. We weren't exactly the 8th Flying Training Command Band, but we got the job done.

A short distance away was a prisoner of war camp, filled with Rommel's Afrika Korps men who had been captured. While we were in good physical condition, we were no match for those guys.

They all had jobs to do on their base, and they did just enough to stay in tip-top shape. They were all blue-eyed and blonde-headed and were as bronze as if they had been cast. Since there was no base band, we went to their base every Friday and played retreat. We also played some marches, and when we were marching down the last street where the biggest concentration of Germans were, we played "Right in *der Fuhrer's* Face" with much gusto and lots of the noise made during that song.

This place is in the middle of nowhere, and no one was too worried about escaped prisoners. Every once in a while one would get away, but it was a hell of a long way to Mexico, and they would voluntarily return. That part of Oklahoma is flat, sparsely populated, and you can see for miles.

The semester ended, and we had to move on. We were to go to what was called on-the-line training, but they didn't know where. One of our guys, Jim Davenport from Pittsburg, came down with spinal meningitis on Friday, and he died on Saturday morning. They formed an honor guard of three or four of his closest friends, and took him home to Pittsburg.

The rest of us boarded a train and headed for Frederick Air Force Base in Frederick, Oklahoma. We were, from the moment Jim got sick, quarantined. No one who worked on the train could see or talk to us, and when we stopped at any place, we were not allowed off the train or out of our individual cars. When we got to Frederick, we were restricted to our area, and no one got within 30 or 40 feet of us. When we went to the mess hall, the food was on the serving line, but there was no one to serve us. We got our trays, filled them, ate the food, and had to wash our trays and silverware in G. I. cans which were placed at the door as we left.

That went on for the entire incubation period of spinal meningitis; I think it was three or four weeks. During the period we were quarantined, our days were the same, day after day. We were the only group on our base that stood reveille. After reveille, we went to the mess hall for breakfast. After breakfast a sergeant from special services got on a physical training stand about 30 feet from the nearest of us. He led us through calisthenics for an hour or so. Then we played basketball until lunch.

After lunch, we marched around the field we had been in all morning That lasted for a couple of hours, after which we played basketball until it was time to eat, about 4:30 or 5:00. We were the first to eat at every meal, so they could get us out of the way. We were very happy people when our quarantine was lifted.

At night we listened to radio, played cards, and tried to learn Morse code. Most of us could sound the alphabet, and even if you weren't interested, you had to learn from all the dit and dot that was going on.

Our base was a twin-engine advanced training base, and in the 18 months I was there, we went from UC-78's to B-25's to B-26's to A-26's.

When we first got there, we were to stay 30 to 90 days to get familiar with aircraft. Then, we would start our cadet training. That 30 days lasted 18 months.

The war was breaking rather fast, and the government didn't know if it was going to need any more flying officers. They didn't want to release us because we might be needed, so they kept us around as handymen doing whatever we could to help the war effort.

I got drafted into the band to play a baritone horn. The band director, a master sergeant, had played that horn before he was made director. So he was most unhappy with me when he didn't hear me play the solo the baritone had on the "Star Spangled Banner." I had been in the band two or three weeks when he discovered silence on that solo. He was even more perturbed when he found I didn't have any music and had not told him. Our marching band had almost no rehearsals. The band was, however, broken into three or four big swing bands which played at the Officers Club, the NCO club, the base dance hall, and one in Section I, the black service men's section. Since I was not a member of any of those bands, I was free most of the time. What an ideal job.

Dick Van Dyke was a member of our group, and he was always putting together a show or a band. Back then he was more of a magician than a comedian, and the two of us put together a band for a little while for the Officers Club. It wasn't very good and didn't last too long.

We were all air force unassigned. Until we were assigned to something, we couldn't be transferred. The band was transferred to the South Pacific, and unless I was willing to be assigned to the band, I couldn't go. I wasn't, and I didn't.

Next I was given to the instrument shop which repaired, replaced, installed, and checked the instruments on the planes. That was much more interesting, and I enjoyed it. I could start some of the aircraft and taxi them to the compass rose, which we used to check the heading of the compasses. That was as near as I got to flying, with the exception of the eight or ten hours we flew cubs when we were at Northwestern State Teachers College in Alva.

My cousin Billy Millis was a flight instructor at a twin-engine advanced base at Altus, Oklahoma which wasn't too far away. He flew over to see me several times and flew over once to get checked out in the A-26, which was about as hot as any plane we had then. On that occasion we flew to Oklahoma City and got in touch with Cotton Neer, another Martinsville serviceman who was stationed, I think, at Tinker Field. On the way back to Frederick, we were losing altitude slowly, and we were flying at nearly 400 mph, which was fighter pilot stuff. I was most impressed.

I never really knew when Bill was coming; he'd just fly in and have someone get me. It always felt good when I got a call or a person came by to say, "There's a Captain Millis to see you at transient." We didn't have a lot in common to talk about, and certainly we were moving in quite different circles. I was a private first class, and he was a captain. But it was really good to see someone from home, especially a cousin.

CHAPTER 21

Hiding a Car and Other Amusements

Frederick is on the Great Plain, had very clean air, and you could see nearly forever. The first night we were there, we looked out over the flat plain and could see a schoolhouse very clearly. We thought it might be a half mile to a mile away, but it was nearly six miles. Most of us were from the Iowa to Ohio patch and were not as used to such clear, dry, air. We never thought we'd like that climate, but we grew to really appreciate it.

We had several dust storms, and when we had really bad ones, the officers would send us out on the line to hold the airplanes down. I often wondered what they thought we could do. In reality, our assignment was to keep the tie-down ropes on each plane tight so they would stay in their place and not bang each other up. After we got into the bigger bomber type planes, we'd check the ropes, then get in the planes and sleep the storm away. But we never lost a plane to a sandstorm.

I have many, many memories of that 18 months, some of which I'd be a cad to relate, and some of which I'm not proud. But that's where I learned to drink whiskey, improved my ability to dance, and improved my ability to communicate with the opposite sex.

While I was stationed there, my brother, Max, and my sister, Marian, drove down to see me. They checked into a local hotel, and their room became headquarters for my friends and me. One of them, a tech sergeant named Riggs, was about the same size as Max. One afternoon they swapped clothes. Max became a tech sergeant, and Riggs put on a suit; we paraded up and down the two or three blocks of Frederick. They didn't stay long, I think three days, but it was a most memorable time.

I got two promotions while I was at Frederick Air Force Base. The first came because I had served for a year and the private first class came automatically. The second, the move to corporal, was because our base was given enough corporals to move every private first class to corporal. That moved my pay all the way up to $66 a month. From that, I had to deduct the $7.50 for my war bond; the $5, I think it was, for my insurance; and the $2.50 for laundry.

The girl I was dating was Ila Faye Sisk – she was employed as a telephone operator – and we generally had all the money we needed. Night life was rather quiet in Frederick. The local bar served only beer, chili, and hamburgers. It had been the Chevrolet garage until there were no more Chevies, and it became the Duration Bar.

One serviceman had an American Austin. I don't know how much it weighed, but four of us could pick it up and carry it away. Many nights we'd move his car and try to hide it. He took a dim view of that, but he never knew who was playing games with him. One night on the base, some guys put his car in the ditch that surrounded our barracks. The ditch was about ten feet across and seven feet deep. It took him all day to find enough people to help him get it out.

Any group of servicemen is a diverse group. One man who made a big impression on me was a man named Harry Stravens. Harry was about 6' 3" tall and weighed 155. He grew up in the mountains of North Carolina and was what I had pictured as a hillbilly. He said he got drafted when he came down from the mountains to get sugar to make moonshine. He hadn't known we were at war.

The grocer that had always sold him sugar told him he had to have sugar stamps. Harry didn't know what they were or where to get them. They sent him to the ration board. When he got to the ration board, they couldn't identify him, and they sent him to the draft board. When he got to the draft board, they registered him and drafted him at the same time. He didn't get any sugar, but he did get into the army air corps.

Harry was married and told about getting married. His wife was named Mae; her father was Luther. Harry went to Luther and asked him for Mae's hand. Luther said, "You can have her, Harry, but wait until the kid grows up."

Harry said, "You don't understand, Luther, we got to get married."

Luther said, "Well, hell, then, Harry, take her." I asked Harry how old she was when this happened, and he told me she was nearly 14. When I met her she was 23, and she had three children, the youngest of whom had started school. Harry was about 35.

Harry was a poker player who was totally unpredictable. You were never sure if he was putting you on or was dumb as a post. He never threw away a pair even if they were two's or three's or four's. Many times he'd stay until it was time to show, and then he'd say, "All I got is three little two's or three little four's," and he won many pots from the serious gamblers.

Another friend of mine was Jack Whittaker. Jack was from Fort Worth, and his dad owned O. C. Whittaker Pipe Line Construction Company. He took me home with him one weekend, and the thing that impressed me the most was the saddles he had on sawhorses in his bedroom. There were two of them, and they had silver all over them. He was justifiably proud of them, and he said they were used in fancy parades and at shows.

Jack was a gambler. One night he came by and asked me if I had any money. I think I had about $5, and I gave it to him. He played blackjack all night and won $600. The next night he got in a poker game and won $800. He went to town and found a car he wanted to buy, but the seller wanted $2,000. He put a $600 deposit on the car, brought the rest of the money back to the base and got in another game. He lost it all. He went back to town, got his deposit, brought it back to the base, and lost it. In three days he had run $5 up to more than $1,400 and lost it all.

There were fun times, too. We had a rubber-tread crawler tractor much like a Caterpillar that was used to pull the planes around. On more than one night, when they weren't flying night missions, I'd get on it and drive it up and down the apron, pulling on both the sticks at the same time, then releasing them and accelerating. You could make that big thing rock like a boat in four- or five-foot seas.

Another thing we used to do was steal jeeps. If someone left his jeep with the key in it, and left it unattended, it likely would be gone when he returned for it. We'd play jeep tag and see how far we could jump over the little ramps near the runways. When we were through with them, we always put them back where we picked them up. As far as I know, none of us ever got into serious trouble for this frolicking.

I got some of my first understandings of human nature there. We had a captain from Detroit named Madacek who wanted to improve the efficiency of the base. He put us on what he called alert. If you were assigned an aircraft, it had to be in flying status. If it wasn't, you had to be with that plane until it was. Even if it took 48 hours, you were on duty until it reached flying status. If all your planes were on flying status, you were off duty. I was an instrument technician, and if we had any planes with instrument problems, we were on duty. If our board was clear, we were off. If we had any uncleared jobs on the board, we were on duty. This approach must have had much merit, because while both the north and south flight lines had about the same number of planes, our end was flying more than 75% of the training missions. And we were off duty much more than the guys at the other end of the flight line. This was my first exposure to incentive-directed results, and I was most impressed.

I even ended up working for a time as a methods engineer, which depended upon incentives to inspire employees.

There was a master sergeant named Halperin who had served in World War I with Doolittle, Mitchell, and those early fliers, and knew them all. A short time after Madacek had instituted his plan, the colonel who was in charge of the line was talking to him about the results. The colonel, whose name was Noakes, asked Madacek how Halperin treated him as his commanding officer. Madacek answered that he'd be happy if Halperin treated him as an equal, much less a commanding officer.

This same master sergeant went down to Love Field, where the headquarters of our flying training command was, to see about getting his son-in-law, who was a colonel and being rotated from the Pacific Theatre, stationed at Love Field. He was successful. There just has to be something about human nature there.

My cousin Bill was stationed at Altus, Oklahoma, a town about 30 or 40 miles from Frederick. That base had no band, and we did. The commanding general of our flying training command was going to make an inspection of the Altus base, so they trucked our band there so we could play for the general. We marched and played past the reviewing stand, and when we got to the appointed spot, we quit playing and formed a double row beside the tarmac. I had never had to stand at attention for long periods of time, and I didn't know that if you locked your knees tightly, the odds were you couldn't last long. At any rate, I was standing there doing my best to look both important and soldierly, when the general's car approached. I knew I wasn't going to make it and told the trombone player to my left that I was going down. He told the man on my right – I don't remember who he was – to grab my arm. When the general passed, I was being held up by these two men and was about as limp as a dishrag. As he passed, the general said, "Get that man out of the hot sun." They did, and it ended the band's participation in the festivities.

On the 38th anniversary of the army air corps, we had a celebration on our base. They flew in a B-29, and parked it at the end of the runway. We could walk around it, but could not enter it. We had heard about this giant plane, and now we could see it. It was almost unbelievably big. It stayed a few hours and then left, I assume, to go to another air base for stimulating admiration.

At the time we were flying B-26's out of our base. The B-26 was nicknamed the flying prostitute because it had no visible means of support. When it was first designed, it was called the bumblebee, because neither it nor the bumblebee seemed to have broad enough wingspans to support flight. I don't remember at what speed it stalled, but it was considerably higher than most planes of its day, and most pilots took nearly all the runway in taking off and a great percentage of it in landing.

On this day, one of our instructors was intent on showing how safe the plane really was by taking off on a short runway. He had a B-26 at the end of the runway, brakes fully on, and engines revved up as far as he safely could. The plane was literally jumping up and down when he finally released the brakes. The plane started down the runway and gained speed much faster than normal. When he was about a third of the way down the runway, he pulled the wheels up and raised the nose. The plane climbed about 10 or 12 feet in the air, and he put it into a slight glide to gain speed. When he finally had safe airspeed, his props weren't 18 inches off the ground. That doesn't sound like any big deal, but I can assure you that those of us who saw it were greatly impressed and will never forget it. We also had some flyovers by some fighter pilots, which impressed those of us who longed to do that too.

Let me tell you about a couple of funny things that I witnessed while at Frederick. At one point we were training French cadets. Most had pretty good ability to speak and understand English, but some didn't. They were flying B-25's, the plane that Billy Mitchell took off from a carrier in and bombed Tokyo with. There was a movie made about that air raid.

When the cadets were able to fly without instructors, many of them wanted to duplicate taking off a carrier. Most of them made it, but some didn't. Those planes that didn't make it had a trip to PLM hanger for, at least, new props. One cadet made his final approach without his wheels down. There was a loud buzz that came on if your airspeed approached stall and the wheels were up. The tower kept trying to tell him his wheels were up, and could not get a response. He landed with his wheels up. The plane stayed on the runway, but didn't go too far. When they came to get the plane, they put inflatable bags under the wings, blew them up, put the wheels in down-and-locked position, and the wheels went down and locked. When they asked the cadet why he didn't respond to their instructions about the wheels, he replied that he couldn't hear what they were saying because of all the noise that damned buzzer was making.

As I noted before, while I was there, we went from UC 78's, which were referred to as double breasted cubs, to B-25's, to B-26's, to A-26's. The last three were real fighting planes, and the A-26 was state of the art.

The UC-78's had wood frames and were covered with fabric. The wheels on them retracted, but not fully. About half the wheel was still exposed when they were up. One day a ferry pilot who was bringing a plane to us flew it into the runway with the wheels up. When she stopped, the props were about two feet long and very splintered. She forgot to lower the wheels. The only thing that was damaged was the props, and that happened more than once when those planes were utilized.

At Altus, where my cousin was a flight instructor, they had another instructor named George Gobel. George had been an entertainer before he had entered the air corps, and became one of our country's most famous comedians after the war. Bill told me a story about George concerning an accident he had on the apron. There was a line of planes waiting to take off, and George's plane nipped a bit off the tail of the plane ahead of him. Of course, when accidents like that happen, they're reviewed. When the review was being held, the board asked George what happened. His answer was he didn't know. He was just sitting there and that plane in front just backed into him. That answer was so unique that he got into no trouble for the problem.

CHAPTER 22

Separation

About the middle of October I called home and was talking to my parents. When I was talking to my dad, he asked me if I wanted the store after I was discharged. Of course, I told him yes.

He couldn't have known at that time—I didn't know either—that I would be discharged in two weeks. I was sent to Chanute Field for separation.

As I was going through the chow line there, I noticed that one of the servers was a sergeant who had been a friend of mine at Frederick, proving once again that it's a small world. I held up the line a bit while we chatted, and he told me a story about Chanute Field. It is an old, established base for the flying army, and as such was in the forefront of many innovations.

At one end of the base was an old B-19. It was our bomber when we entered the war. It cruised at about 115 m.p.h. Someone wondered if we could mount a cannon in an airplane and decided to find out, mounting a 75 mm cannon in the plane, then taking the plane up and firing the cannon. The result was most unexpected. The plane stopped in midair. Fortunately, the altitude was sufficient for the plane to recover, and the pilot was able to land the plane safely. The surprise was what the firing had done to the fuselage. The skin of the plane was made so that each piece of aluminum lapped the one before it by between a quarter and a half of an inch. Then they were riveted to each other and the frame. After the cannon fired, many of those sheets were butted, and the rivets were u-shaped. That's how the U.S. Army Air Corps found out that in order to mount cannons on planes, they needed far better recoil mechanisms than they had.

❊ ❊ ❊ ❊ ❊ ❊

It had taken me several weeks to qualify to be a cadet. Getting out was much easier. The last interview I had was for the army air force reserve, which I joined for three years. I did so because I hadn't been in the service long enough to be eliminated from the draft list.

The whole procedure took less than two days. I decided that life, like the service, can be a lot easier getting out than it is getting in.

I hitchhiked home — about 100 miles — and walked into the store. To my great surprise, there were no Stanfields there. Ghandi McClellan was the new owner and proprietor.

I went on home and asked Dad why. He stated the reason simply: "There have to be easier ways to make a living."

I knew he was right and that I had to accept the fact that this part of my life was over.

The rest was up to me.

THE END

STANFIELD'S STORE IN THE 1940'S – MARTINSVILLE, ILLINOIS

From left: My father, O. R. Stanfield, holding the Blunk child; Wilbur Deahl; the butcher, George Storzham; my uncle, Jim Stanfield; Mrs. Blunk; and Mildred Wells.

Printed in the United States
90040LV00004B/406-453/A